I0410041

<u>INTRODUCTION</u>

This workbook is especially designed for dance-fitness instructors who are teaching independently and are looking for ways to promote and market their classes. It can be used by those who teach Zumba Fitness®, BodyJam®, Jazzercise®, Cardio Funk, Hip Hop, Groove, Salsaerobics, Dance Trance, Nia, Balletone®, Ballerobica, Tap to Burn or any other variety of dance-fitness classes. Containing lots of marketing ideas, strategies and action steps, this book will help you fill your classes and build your business.

This workbook is divided into two parts. Part One is The Basics – steps you should take when establishing your business and starting classes. Part Two is Special Events – things you can do, both online and off, to attract more students.

THE BASICS

YOUR BUSINESS IDENTITY

Your business identity is a combination of what you offer, your philosophy and you as a person. It is important to have this defined when you begin your marketing and promotion efforts. It will especially help you as you design and produce print materials, press releases, web pages and online profiles.

A description of my business in a few sentences:

_____

_____

_____

_____

What to expect at one of my classes:

_____

_____

_____

_____

_____

Marketing Basics for Dance-Fitness Instructors

A short bio or "about me" paragraph:

_____

_____

_____

_____

_____

What makes you and your classes unique and different?

_____

_____

_____

Make a list of words that describe your business and what you offer. These keywords can be used in articles, press releases, web pages, profiles, online descriptions, etc. Include terms that people might use to search for your classes online, as well as geographic terms related to your location.

_____

_____

_____

_____

_____

Marketing Basics for Dance-Fitness Instructors

☐ I have a name for my business that reflects what I offer.

☐ If necessary, I have registered the name with my city or town.

☐ I have a phone number dedicated to my business.

☐ I have a tag-line or catch-phrase for my business.

YOUR FACILITY AND SIGNS

Your facility is obviously a great way to market to the public, whether it is something you own, lease or a space that you rent by the hour.

☐ I have a sign at my facility for my business. It is either a permanent or temporary sign, but may also include a banner, poster in the window or letters on window glass.

☐ I have a roadside or sidewalk sign to attract traffic passing by.

☐ I have signage on my vehicle to attract attention on the road and in parking lots. The sign is either detailed onto the vehicle, a magnetic sign that is removable, or a bumper sticker.

☐ I have signs in other locations around town to direct people to my facility.

What you can include on signs:

The name of your business

Your logo or tag-line

Contact info including phone, email and/or website

Short description of what you offer

Current offerings

Benefits of your classes

An incentive, discount or special offer

PRINT and PROMO MATERIALS

Print marketing materials include any kind of paper product that you will pass out in order to promote your classes. While you don't need all of the items below at one time, this will give you an idea of different strategies you can try. Use the paragraphs and sentences that you wrote in the Business Identity section to help you design your print materials, utilizing the services of a graphic designer if necessary.

☐ I have a logo for my business.

☐ I give away free T-shirts, pens, keychains, etc. to students to gain more exposure in the community.

☐ I have designed graphic ads ready for newspapers and other publications.

Where to place your graphic ads:

In newspapers, magazines and other local publications

In church bulletins

In school newsletters and yearbooks

In organization newsletters such as Health Centers, Insurance Companies, Senior Centers,

Community Centers, Local business organizations, Military base newsletters

On placemats at local restaurants

In Community theater programs

Other ideas: _____

☐ I have business cards and hand them out to anyone I meet.

☐ I have brochures/take-aways that describe my offerings in more detail.

☐ I have coupons that offer a free class or discount.

☐ I have fliers that describe what I offer and have an incentive along with

my contact information.

<u>Where to distribute your print materials:</u>

At all of your classes, events, demos, fundraisers and offerings

On telephone poles, community bulletin boards, bus stops

On top of pizza boxes from your local pizza delivery place

In bags at local grocery stores and shops, or at the checkout counter

As an insert in your local newspaper or other publication

YOUR PERSON

One of the best ways to advertise is you. You never know when you're going to meet someone who could turn out to be a student. Practicing talking about your basic description of your classes and having print materials on you at all times will insure you're ready to invite anyone that shows interest.

- [ ] I have clothing with my business information on it to inspire people to ask me about my classes.
- [ ] I talk to people every day about my classes.

STUDENTS

Attracting new students is always a priority but you can also use current and former students as a way to spread the word about your classes.

Who are your classes designed for?

Age _____

Gender _____

Physical Ability _____

Geographic locations _____

_____

Income level _____

What other interests or hobbies might potential students have?

_____

_____

_____

_____

_____

Where do potential students go in town, socially and to do business?

_____

_____

_____

_____

_____

☐ I register my students and collect their name, address, phone, email, birthday and how they heard about me.

☐ I track my students' birthdays and acknowledge them with cards, gifts, a class incentive or other special offer.

☐ My students know my website, phone and contact info because it is on my receipts/paperwork, present at my facility and I tell them frequently. They can easily pass on my info to an interested friend.

☐ I stay in contact with former students and occasionally invite them back.

☐ I give my current students "free trial class" coupons to hand out to their friends.

LOCAL MEDIA

Local media includes newspapers and publications as well as TV and radio outlets.

☐ I have listed my classes in my local newspaper's calendar of events.

☐ I have published a graphic ad in the newspaper.

☐ I have invited a local reporter to visit my class/event to do an article.

☐ I send press releases to local publications when I hold special events.

☐ I am listed in the Yellow Pages (and the online version).

☐ I have an ad on the local radio station.

☐ I am on Cable Access television, either the bulletin board and/or a show.

☐ I advertise at the local movie theater, either on screen or in the facility.

THE INTERNET

There are many ways to market your business online. To begin, you should have the basics including a website, email and accounts on various social networks.

What to include on your pages and profiles:

Your name and contact information including email and phone number

A basic description of your classes

Some photos of you, your facility and/or your classes(make sure to tag people!)

A special incentive or discount

Videos of sample classes, choreography, a welcome and invite, etc.

A link to where they can sign-up for your email newsletter

☐ I have a website about my business and classes. It is optimized for search engines with keywords and relevant content.

☐ I have an email address for my business.

☐ I have an email list or newsletter so I can contact my students and potential new students as a group.

☐ I always include a "Forward to a Friend/Share This" button in my emails and my blog posts so students can easily pass on my class info.

☐ I have a Facebook Page for my business.

☐ I have a Twitter account for my business where I post current offerings, invites to classes and links to resources.

☐ I am listed in online directories, including locally-based ones.

Some online directories to consider:

Manta.com

GooglePlaces

MerchantCircle.com

InsiderPages.com

CitySearch.com

Local.yahoo.com

You can also Search for "online business directory" and research the results to see if you want to list on them

You may also want to search for directories with search terms such as "fitness instructor directory, dance teacher directory" or other similar terms

☐ I regularly publish ads on Classified Ad sites.

Good Classified Ad Sites to List on:

Craigslist.org

EbayClassifieds.com (formerly Kijiji)

Webcosmo.com

Local classified sites may do better to attract students than nationwide sites

☐ I have accounts on Calendar and Event websites and regularly list my

classes there.

Calendar and Event Websites to Include Your Classes On:

OLX.com

Socialweb.net

Eventful.com

Make sure to research any local ones too!

☐ I am listed on online review sites.

Online Review Sites:

Yelp.com

MeasuredUp.com

Maps.Google.com (technically a map site but has reviews available)

How to Get Students to Post Reviews:

Ask!

Offer an incentive if they post a review such as a free class or gift

Include links to the review site in all your email correspondence

Place a link to the review site on your website and social networking pages

☐ I have accounts on business networking sites.

Business Networking Sites:

LinkedIn.com

MeetUp.com

Upspring.com

☐ I have coupons offered on online coupon sites.

☐ I have listed my information on any online organizations that I belong to that have websites and member directories such as Zumba.com, IDEA, or other organizations I have certified and trained with.

ONLINE VIDEOS

Videos are a great way to introduce yourself online and promote your classes.

They can be searched and found online by potential students but you can also use them to stay connected with your current students.

☐ I have sample class videos.

☐ I have an instructor introduction video.

☐ I have instructional videos.

☐ I have a basic promotional video/commercial about my business.

Where to put your online videos:

Your website

Your social networking profiles such as Facebook and LinkedIn

YouTube and other video sharing sites

In emails sent to your email list and new students

What to include in the description of the video:

Your website and contact information

Search keywords such as your location, zip code, city, county, etc.

Internet Advertising and Promotion

☐ I advertise on Facebook.

☐ I advertise and sponsor groups on MeetUp.com.

☐ I have a Google Adwords account and place ads on relevant websites.

☐ I have a list of online press release sites and regularly send out press

releases about current offerings.

SPECIAL EVENTS

LOCAL NETWORKING

One of the best ways to get more students is by reaching out into your community and networking. This includes getting to know the owners of other local businesses as well as offering those businesses and organizations a taste of your classes. Sometimes meeting you in person is the first step towards deciding to try one of your classes. You may even find that the business or organization wants to hire you to teach regular classes with them. You can find businesses and organizations through the local newspapers, online searches, asking friends or even the yellow pages. For each of the businesses/organizations you list in this section, jot down some ideas of how you could potentially network with them.

How to network

Offer free trial classes

Discounts for members

Invite the owner

Place coupons at their facility

Do a free demo at their facility or for their employees

Offer to do a fundraiser for them

Set up a booth or kiosk showcasing your classes

Local health and fitness organizations or businesses:

Include gyms, fitness centers, health insurance companies, weight-loss groups, waiting rooms at medical centers, doctors, fitness fairs, health expos, hospitals

_____

_____

_____

_____

_____

_____

Local beauty-related organizations and businesses:

Include spas, hair and nail salons, hairdressers, fashion consultants, etc.

_____

_____

_____

_____

Local vacation-related businesses and organizations:

Include ski lodges, hotels, conference centers, travel agencies, etc.

_____

_____

_____

_____

Local business organizations:

Include the Chamber of Commerce or other business associations

_____

_____

_____

_____

Local businesses and organizations that deal with relocation and new moves:

Include realtors, moving companies, storage, etc.

_____

_____

_____

_____

Local stores and malls that sell to your potential students:

_____

_____

_____

_____

Local city or town departments and military organizations:

Include the recreation department, senior center, library, veterans association, military base, fire/police department, etc.

_____

_____

_____

_____

Local holiday events in my community:

Holiday walks, Trick-or-Treating, Labor Day Sales, etc.

_____

_____

_____

_____

Local teams and sports events:

_____

_____

_____

_____

Local fairs and gatherings for the community:

Include any regular community events, fairs, farmer's markets, celebrations,

parades, festivals and more

_____

_____

_____

_____

Local social-activity groups:

Include singles' groups, mothers' groups, playgroups, young professionals, etc.

_____

_____

_____

_____

Local schools, colleges and learning institutions:

Include schools, PTOs, colleges, adult learning, sororities, preschools, career days

_____

_____

_____

_____

Local businesses with large numbers of employees:

Contact the HR department to see if they may want to offer something for them

_____

_____

_____

_____

Local religious organizations and churches:

Include church bazaars and fairs you could get involved with

_____

_____

_____

_____

Ideas for other local businesses I could network with:

Refer back to your ideal student and where they congregate locally

_____

_____

_____

_____

PROMOTIONAL EVENTS

At all promotional events you should be collecting addresses and emails of anyone attending so you can send them more information about your classes at a future point. You should also send out a press release about any special events you offer, both on and offline. Take photos at the events and post on your web pages and in newsletters, too.

☐ Bring a friend. Your current students bring a friend to class for some sort of incentive.

☐ Bring a friend to Facebook. Ask your Facebook friends to refer someone to your page and if that person "likes" your page they both get an incentive.

☐ Free demonstration of your class at an event such as a charity fundraiser, race, fair, community event, school function or half-time show.

☐ An Open House where you invite the public to your facility, distribute print materials and collect names for your mailing list.

☐ A Fundraiser for a local or national organization, done at their facility or yours. Fundraisers are a great way to get some free publicity and news attention while helping others.

Incentives:

Free or discounted classes

T-shirts, hats, bags, water bottles, etc.

The choice of music during one class

A routine choreographed to their favorite song

A dance/fitness CD or DVD

Tracking What is Working

Keeping track of what is working will help you determine where to put your efforts in the future. A simple way to do this is with a table such as the one below. It assumes that you are either asking new students and others that inquire where they heard about your classes and/or you are asking for this information on registration forms.

Date	Description of Promotional Event or Marketing Strategy You Tried	Resulting Inquiries or New Students

www.ingramcontent.com/pod-product-compliance
Lightning Source LLC
Chambersburg PA
CBHW060815290526
45792CB00005BB/1662